Contents

    Preface ....

1   Do we have the right str...

2   Are we doing the right things?........................5

3   Is the total cost of ownership applied?........................8

4   Are we buying what we need?........................10

5   How are savings measured? 12

6   Are we working capital aware?........................14

7   Does procurement really control spend? 16

8   Do we pay on time? 18

9   What is the potential for reducing purchase cost?.....20

10   Do we have the right skills? 22

    Contacts 25

Preface

This booklet tries to answer a few simple questions for a new leader in a procurement function. What questions should you ask? What answers should you expect? When should you smell a rat and what should you do about it.

These days so many people try to dress up procurement as a hugely complicated function. The result has been masses of detailed publications on a myriad of subjects that make it difficult for the uninitiated to get a broad grasp of the subject. So if you are looking for a technical manual, stop reading now. If you want a holistic overview that might be useful in getting a perspective for the functions total operations, please continue.

This not meant to be a technical manual and therefore tries to avoid, or at least simply explain, the technical jargon nowadays used by procurement specialists.

I will apologise in advance where I have failed in that aim and I hope you find the content useful to your procurement role.

1 Do we have the right structure?

There have been many debates over the years to determine the right structure for procurement in different organisations. The real answer is that there is no right answer. The right structure will be determined by what your organisation does, in how many places is it done and with how many people is it being done. The top three that people usually go for are centralised, decentralised and centre-led.

The initial instinct of many organisations is to centralise as much as possible. In theory this should allow the procurement process to be more closely controlled creating process efficiencies. It should also allow for greater synergies to be found through bulk buying, specification control and having a group of real experts to make sure that they are getting the best value for your company. In high end engineering companies this structure is commonly utilised. It allows for extremely tight specification control that is vital to the safe operating of certain manufactured goods. An example would be aerospace. We don't see many planes dropping out of the sky for technical reasons and this is not just about great engineering. It is also about having centralised procurement teams that are aligned with the engineers to ensure that specifications are being met, proper certifications are being obtained and the right negotiation techniques are being applied. But it can also lead to massive bureaucracies, especially when dealing with areas of non-core spend. This tends to happen because the detailed process that might be required to safely procure part of aircraft engine will probably be too severe to safely procure pencils. The result can be massive inefficiency and a stakeholder community that will try to avoid proper procurement processes at every opportunity.

For this reason many stakeholders will argue in favour of a decentralised model. This model has the advantage of being closer to the internal customer, especially in an organisation with multiple locations. All local preferences can be easily catered for and there can even be large variations in process depending on the needs and views of the local stakeholders. However, this kind of model usually wastes vast amounts of value since it is difficult to consolidate spend, difficult to control purchase specifications and bordering on impossible to control the proliferation of suppliers that will inevitably occur.

A better way forward can be the centre-led model. In this case there is a centralised team of procurement specialists. They work with stakeholders to develop the specifications and then make sure that the company gets the best deal based on those specifications. They also organise the process so it is as efficient for the end user as possible without losing purchasing control. For example, in years gone by it was necessary to fill in a purchase order to buy pencils, get it authorised, send it to procurement, wait for procurement to do their magic and several weeks later you might get a pencil. In a centre-led scenario, you know you want a pencil, the supplier and purchase price is predetermined by our procurement specialists, you order directly with the supplier (using catalogues, P-Cards, call-off orders) and the goods arrive as quickly as the supplier can get them to your desk. This can work very well for areas of non-core spend, but the criticism is that there are certain areas of spend where this could not work effectively. An example would be commodities, where prices are continually fluctuating and there are more complex ways of buying, e.g. price hedging.

Often the right solution is a mixture of centralised and centre-led. While at a company that made industrial level copper cables, 70% of spend was on copper and aluminium, another 20% various materials required for casings and the remainder on local services such as facilities, travel and transport. Their solution was a centralised team who only bought copper and aluminium and a centre-led team to cover all the other areas of spend. This made good use of resources who were spread all over Europe, but who each had different specialities. So metals buyers were located at head office, while all the other centre-led buyers were based in their home countries (UK, Netherlands, Finland, and Germany) but creating deals for the entire group. This avoided the need for a large centralised bureaucracy, allowed the necessary synergies to come together in data sharing and leverage of spending power and finally led to a lean, cost effective and efficient purchase process.

2 Are we doing the right things?

One of the burdens of leadership is that your staff are very likely to give you positive answers for most things. The ones to pinpoint are those who are new to the job and those about to leave. The new staff member will have no mental baggage, but also lacks experience of the department. So while you may get clearer opinions, those opinions can lack relevance to the situation. On the other hand, speak to those who intend to leave and they will often be disgruntled on certain points. It is worth listening to these views, even if you don't agree with them, since there is usually a grain of truth somewhere in their stories.

When it comes to identifying savings get ready for a number of stock answers. We can't do anything since company x is the only one that can supply at the required level of quality. The price is driven by the market and there is nothing we can do. It would cost too much to certify a new supplier even though we might get a lower price. That supplier is on a three year deal, so there is nothing we can do in the meantime. And the list continues. There is always something that can be done. It's just a question of whether the effort is worthy of the potential return.

One thing to do is accompany your top sourcing managers on their next visits to key suppliers. Supplier relationships can sometimes become too comfortable and this will have the effect of limiting you leverage. Vital questions can remain unanswered. Key information can be out of date. It is important that sourcing managers are always questioning the stakeholders' needs and suppliers' capability of delivering to those needs. When these probes are continually being sent in a constructive manner, it ensures that expectations are up to date, that full leverage is being sought with the supplier and often benefits the supplier by being more nimble to customer requirements.

Visit some of your company's sites and look for some simple things. Different types of photocopier, paper towels, facilities management, security guards, forklifts, laptops are all good clues that there are still opportunities to consolidate spend. These might not sound like big ticket items, but they can be relatively straight-forward savings compared to core expenditure items. It is very common that procurement organisations focus on the core expenditure items and tend to ignore the lesser items of spend. While this approach can make sense in order to manage the business' expectation on gross profit, it can result in a multitude of lost opportunities to improve the bottom line.

Speak to your internal stakeholders to understand how procurement works with their departments. If the opinion is that procurement are the guys who make our life difficult by forcing us to use the wrong suppliers, or cause excessive paperwork, or don't get the best prices, don't necessarily jump to the conclusion that procurement is getting everything wrong. It might just be that these people were used to doing their own thing and now they are under some form of control. But the opinions should be tested.

At one client, the procurement department had set up a car rental deal that looked like it should be delivering massive savings. However, the spend lists did not show any significant expenditure with the chosen supplier. So we called several branches of the car rental agency, trying to rent a car on the negotiated rates. The answer we continually got was that there were no cars available on that rate. So the choice was to rent a car on their standard (and expensive) rates or switch to another supplier. Although the deal had been agreed, it was not capable of execution since the rental company was not prepared to lose money on the deal. The result was that the client was paying over the odds with other suppliers. This along with some other examples was clear evidence that non-core procurement was not pulling its weight in the organisation. The resulting programme delivered sizeable savings in a number of spend categories in the following twelve months.

There is also an important point about process efficiency. At a major engineering company everyone we came in contact with would complain about the bureaucratic process that procurement put you through every time you needed to complete an order. In this case, the requisitioner needed to fill out a purchase requisition, get it signed, send it to procurement, who often took weeks to complete the order. As a result people tried to avoid the process. They would either contact the supplier directly and then the purchase requisition would be required once the suppliers invoice arrived in accounts payable. Or they would buy smaller items through their personal expense accounts. There was a one size fits all purchase process meaning that the same process was used to by capital equipment and stationery. There was no use of purchase cards or catalogues that would have made the process easier for the requisitioner, cut out all the paperwork and delays and ensured compliance with deals negotiated by procurement.

3 Is the total cost of ownership applied?

While working with a packaging company that used aluminum foil as its main raw material in its plants in Germany and the US, we were told that all foil was being sourced from Germany since the cost was deemed to be lower in cost and the quality was better than similar materials that could be sourced in the US. So we spoke to the suppliers, who happened to be two divisions of the same multinational and this confirmed that while the material quality was identical, the unit cost was cheaper for the German material. However, when the transport and customs cost were included, the cost to the US plant of buying the German material was considerably higher. Further investigation revealed that the reason this had happened was that the US plant had been set up as a clone of the German plant, including the complete supply chain. No one had ever seriously questioned this circumstance due to the lack of local procurement expertise in the US plant and the lack of procurement knowledge at head office. This presented an obvious opportunity to re-source the material from the US and reduce the total cost being paid.

But there are other factors in the equation apart from transportation cost or unit price. With so much manufacturing capacity now moved to the Far East, lead times have increased dramatically. The added inventory holding cost didn't matter that much in the past compared to the huge cost differential that existed between say China and Europe or the United States. But years of high domestic inflation and huge increases in commodity prices continue to close that differential. There are even cases now where companies are moving manufacturing back from China as the US and Europe have regained productivity levels. For those who have off-shored manufacturing or supply relationships, this will become an increasing relevant point and managers will need to continually re-evaluate the equation to ensure that they are securing the greatest value for their companies.

Another major area of concern is spare parts and maintenance cost. When at a bread baker, we were reviewing expenditure on conveyor belts. The particular types being used usually had what were called "18 gauge sprockets" and the parts between different manufacturers were largely interchangeable. However, we noticed an increased tendency to use "17 gauge sprocket" conveyor belts. This was because they were nearly 15% cheaper than anything the competition could sell. The sting in the tail was that because there was only one source for spares, maintenance costs were huge compared to other products. The life time cost of the so-called cheaper conveyor belts was more than 20% higher than other products for no perceived increase in efficiency or reliability. This is why it is essential that all capital expenditure processes evaluate their business cases against the full cost of ownership and not just the present value of the capital item. A similar area of concern is reliability. There is no point in having bought the cheapest machine if it breaks down all the time. The opportunity cost in lost production can be very difficult to calculate, but needs to be part of the whole equation. Proper evaluation of the true total costs of acquisition will ensure that real value is being captured, rather than too great a focus on short term or incorrect calculations of savings.

4 Are we buying what we need?

The best way of saving money for your organisation is not to spend anything at all. But if no-one buys anything then nothing will be made or done to service customer requirements. The usual reality is that stakeholders will have demands that may not be in line with customer requirements. If the stakeholder demand is too low, the customer will perceive the end product to be low quality and if the stakeholder demand is too high, the customer may not be prepared to pay the price that that quality would normally deserve.

This is a particular problem for companies engaged in high-end engineering that have extreme sensitivity to safety issues. What we commonly observe is that the need for high specifications starts to creep into other, less critical buying decisions. That is why demand management is a critical tool in your toolkit.

Procurement can be invaluable by working with stakeholders to ensure that specifications are fit for purpose, while not being excessively costly. An associated issue is design proliferation. For example, it used to be common in the aerospace industry that each designer would have their favourite components that might have appeared in the latest engineering magazines. This vastly increased the cost of manufacture, certification made it difficult to change any of these components, leading to increased long term maintenance costs for the customer. These practices have largely disappeared due to the fantastic work done by many procurement professionals in the last 20 years and has established as normal practice that procurement work closely with designers and engineers in these companies.

But similar techniques can be used across other areas of spend to ensure that the best prices are sought from suppliers while stakeholders receive the required service. An example is a client who had contracted out for plant maintenance services. This 24/7 contract had an agreed three hour lead time for emergencies. But no-one had checked to see how far away the nearest supplier depot was located. It turned out that although the technical service was acceptable, the quickest an engineer could get on site was in four hours. This made for an extremely unhappy plant manager.

But procurement's role is not complete at the stage of specification. At one client, the local procurement staff used an RFP to get the best prices on 200 commonly used stationery items. The contract was then awarded to the winning supplier, and the following year expenditure on stationery rose by 27%. It turned out that the contract was to be driven by the supplier's online catalogue but had not been restricted to just the 200 items agreed to in the RFP. People weren't just buying writing pads and pens, but fountain pens, scientific calculators, and even monogrammed brief cases! It was a genuine surprise to everyone what had happened and the supplier had not behaved maliciously. It was just that an important loophole had not been closed. Thankfully, in this case the error was quickly corrected but not after wasting all the savings that the original contract was due to generate.

5 How are savings measured?

This is a tremendously difficult subject. After spending millions on ERP systems around the world most companies still find it difficult to define savings that emanate from procurement. Accountants and department managers can often find it difficult to understand the cost reductions that have been enabled by procurement and how to track them. In many situations this builds a level of distrust between finance departments and procurement, simply because they are unable to properly pinpoint where the saving should be becoming apparent.

The simplest element to measure is the unit cost of an item. This does assume that your company records each item. That might sounds obvious in a manufacturing environment, but where the spend relates to non-core expenditure the item cost is often not recorded. Assuming that unit cost is measured, then it should be a simple process of looking at the difference in price of that item and there's your saving

But then the mix of items that I bought may have changed. So I may have negotiated a price reduction on item A, but because I used less of that item my total saving may be reduced. Equally, if I used more my saving would be increased.

Then what if the price of an item went up by 10% but when I include the cost of transport and maintenance the total cost of ownership actually went down? It can be very difficult to track savings that impact multiple areas of the chart of accounts as a result of a change in one item's costs. This is the part that can frustrate the accountants. They understand where the cost saving was supposed to evidence itself, but how can you firmly establish that the reduction in maintenance or transport cost is attributable to a particular item?

Then there is cost avoidance. For example, the supplier wanted a 5% price increase. We restricted that to a 2% increase. So we saved 3% through cost avoidance. Inflation or commodity price fluctuations will often influence much of our spend, but many procurement departments will use cost avoidance as a simple way to add to their list of savings, without actually negotiating anything. In many cases this may be the correct approach, but cost avoidance savings should always be closely investigated. But to the outside world defining savings in this manner can sound like fiction.

So it is important that procurement can clearly demonstrate to the sceptics exactly where all the measured savings come from, how they have been calculated and the factors that influence that calculation. The good news is that it is possible with today's ERPs to build models that can perform these calculations easily, but they are difficult to construct and even when they are built there is still a major communication effort required to overcome the doubters.

6 Are we working capital aware?

Most procurement organisations are not properly aware of working capital and its implications. Historically, this has largely because most buyers have never been trained about the importance of working capital to their organisation and the part that they can play.

There are many who are totally unaware about working capital and are measured only on direct cost reductions. Many of these folks do not even know what working capital is and when they are initially told their first understanding will be that it is a finance issue. This is a great pity because procurement are the people who need to be most involved in making sure that we agree the right payment terms with suppliers and understand the impact on inventory holding through the deals that the agree with suppliers.

Very few procurement organisations know the true value of working capital to their organisation. For example, what should be the cost of capital applied to any calculation where there is a potential trade-off between terms and price? In most organisations, there will be several answers, most of which are usually incorrect. Most often, the reason for this is that the official cost of capital has not been communicated to anyone. There is also the case where the strategic need for cash for the organisation overrides any calculation. In other words, the organisation is willing to incur extra cost to conserve cash. Again, when this happens there is a reluctance to communicate the fact, causing procurement to behave in a way that is unintentionally against corporate objectives. In one organisation that had a huge cash pile, the company wanted to use that cash pile to extract further discounts from suppliers, i.e. pay quickly in exchange of a settlement discount. Nearly 40% of suppliers, especially small suppliers, signed up to the programme creating nearly €1 million in net savings. However, in another example, buyers were agreeing short terms for discount terms up to 3% on the understanding that this was required for corporate profitability. Unfortunately, it ended up strangling the cash flow of this rapidly expanding business since, at the same time, its customer terms were getting longer and longer.

But who really understands the inventory holding cost of the deals we close? At a diesel engine factory, there were daily meetings to discuss part shortages. The implication of these shortages were unfinished engines cluttering up the factory floor, late deliveries and delayed customer billing. When we reviewed which parts were causing the problem, they were very often very small value parts (nuts, bolts, washers) that had been set up on the ERP system to follow the normal purchase order flow. Because parameters such as lead time, safety stock and order size were all wrong, these parts would be frequently out of stock. The solution was to introduce a two-bin Kanban system (two bins, when one is empty the supplier fills it up) on the factory floor that did away with all the paper work and shortages and got rid of all the unfinished engines, significantly reducing work in process inventories and getting engines billed to the customer at a much greater pace, helping receivables. There are other cases where the solution may be to have consignment stocks or vendor managed inventory. In these cases it is vital that the trade-off between inventory holding and cost is properly understood or, yet again, we could end up unintentionally destroying value.

7 Does procurement really control spend?

The traditional view is that you can be sure that everything is being fully controlled by the procurement process if every purchase is backed by a purchase order. While there is nothing wrong with purchase orders, the statement only represents a partial truth. We need to exclude those types of spend where a traditional purchase order is not appropriate since it is almost impossible to predict the exact requirement, e.g. energy bills. There are cases where a traditional purchase order is not appropriate since we follow a different process to control spend, e.g. purchase cards, catalogues and evaluated receipts. There will also be the incidents of retrospective purchase orders, i.e. the purchase order was completed after the invoice was received. This is a severe malpractice that should be stamped out firmly in every company as we have not only lost control of the spend, but we have also gone through a completely wasteful process to sign off the offence after the fact.

So it is necessary to ask a more exact question. How much spend is controlled by an authorised procurement process? The percentage of spend covered by an authorised process indicates not only the level of influence procurement has over the sourcing of goods and services, but also indicates the level of process compliance in the organisation in general.

One of the most heartbreaking things can be when a procurement organisation has all of these answers, but is unable to enforce compliance in the organisation. This is very common in decentralised organisations where procurement can become resigned to defeat due to the lack of support from senior management. This is also common in relation to non-core spend where various departments and plant managers will have their favourite suppliers who they perceive as providing a better service, better quality or even better prices.

In these cases the onus is on procurement to gain support for compliance by being able to demonstrate that value that is being wasted by these bad practices. The right reports must exist to understand the compliance landscape in fine detail and the value being lost as a result. At one firm, they developed a three strikes process. The first evidence of maverick spend would trigger a reminder to the departmental manager responsible for the purchase. In the second case, a stern warning was given iterating that this was unacceptable behavior and should not be repeated. If there was a third occasion, the invoice would be refused by accounts payable and redirected to the individual for payment and the individual responsible could be sanctioned under the company's disciplinary procedures.

There are cases where the worst offenders can be senior management. And it's a brave person who's going to tell the boss that they are non-compliant. But it is necessary that the process is led from the top. Without visible and sustained leadership on compliance, it is all too easy to drift into bad practices and continue the path of lost value to the organisation.

8 Do we pay on time?

Most procurement professionals have no idea whether their suppliers are paid on time or not. There is usually no reporting on the subject and the only indicator that things may not be going to plan is when the supplier calls looking for payment. And there are many in procurement that continue to be blissfully unaware of why it is important to pay on time. When suppliers are not being paid or are uncertain when payment will happen, this will inevitably increase the risk level of your supply relationship. This in turn will encourage your supplier to increase prices in the longer term. This is different from having longer payment terms. There is very little evidence to suggest that suppliers increase prices due to longer payment terms. But erratic payment patterns mean that your suppliers cannot plan their cash flows and you can become viewed as a risky customer.

The facts are that every company pays late, pays early and pays on time. It's just that the proportion of payments in each category is different for each company. And it is very common that suppliers do not help themselves to get paid. The number one reason why many invoices are paid late is because the invoice was received late. In one case a supplier sent all their invoices for a month in a single box at the end of the month. As a result the invoices could not be processed in time and therefore late payment was very frequent. When asked why the invoices could not be sent on a more frequent basis, the reply was that could not be done as it would increase the cost of postage. So the practice continued.

And the even when the invoice does get to you the cost of an invoice error is massive. At a US retail chain, 23 million invoices were processed each year, mostly electronically. Only 4% of these invoices had some kind of problem, but that required over 200 people to be employed to fix all the errors.

Another issue that comes up often in the UK and especially in the US is float time. This is the practice of paying by cheque and using the slowest possible postage method to get the cheque to the supplier and then having 3 days between the cheque being deposited by the supplier and the bank giving the supplier value for the cheque. Intuitively, it would seem that you can score extra days of cash flow off your supplier that will be to the good of your company. The reality is that if you employ this practice you are usually destroying value for your company, since you have made it more difficult for your treasury department to forecast daily cash requirements for supplier payments. This means that cash buffers must be kept on hand so that cheques will be honoured. This cash could have been invested by your treasury department or could have been used to reduce company debt. Instead it can sit in a zero interest current account. And using cheques also exposes you and your supplier to fraud. There are cases where cheques have been doctored by fraudsters and cashed. So the best thing is to pay electronically since it is better for your supplier, better for your own company's profitability and safer for all parties involved.

To make sure that payments are happening on time solid reporting at a transactional level is required. With today's ERP systems and reporting packages this has become a more straight-forward task, but it still must be done. These reports will make everyone in procurement aware of both the payment profile of their suppliers and help to manage the overall supplier relationship. But if you don't pay your supplier it is likely that you will not have a great relationship.

9 What is the potential for reducing purchase cost?

All procurement managers will have targets and hopefully most of them are being achieved, but if you are the new leader you need to be able to answer some very pointed questions. What is the potential to reduce purchase cost? How long will it take to get to the bottom line? What is the action plan that will be required? What investments will be required to realise this potential? To get the answer right will mean fulfilling the maximum potential of the department's spend profile.

To get the answer reasonably quickly many companies get external help from specialist consultants. The biggest complaint of many companies that have gone down this route is that it took too long, the benefits promised were not necessarily realisable and it was not always clear that the depth of work done had a real relationship to the eventual value proposition. In addition, it can be hard to replicate the consultants work once they are gone, usually meaning that you will be paying external people for what should be the day job rather than specialist expertise or insight.

Assuming the right skills are available, one of the most important things you can do is build a diagnostic tool from the purchase data in your ERP system. Dependent on the quality of the data you should be able to build a model that differentiates between suppliers, products by commodity type, payment profiles and spend volumes. It is common that ERP data can be missing or out of date. An example is commodity groupings. These were usually built when the ERP system was being implemented, so it can happen that they never change after that. If your spend profile has changed, it is possible that the commodity groups are no longer appropriate. Another example is item codes. There are still many companies who only hold inventory data at product family level. So it can be very difficult for procurement to understand the proper product mix within the family.

Projecting savings in each of the categories will depend on a number of elements. The first will be the numbers of suppliers in the category versus the volume of spend. The higher the number of suppliers, the more likely that saving can be obtained by consolidating spend into deals with one or two suppliers. Next will be the length of time since any deal was negotiated. If a deal was only done a few months ago it is less likely to produce saving versus if the deal was done three years ago. Then there is criticality. The less critical the spend the more likely it is that you will have a choice of suppliers and may be able to substitute various suppliers products. And finally there is the commodity itself. If the group is an openly traded commodity such as metals, grain or wood pulp, it is unlikely that you will have enough power to change market pricing. But at the other end of the spectrum there are categories like transport, office supplies, spare parts, facilities management and security where there may be more genuine opportunities.

Once all this is in place, it will be necessary to have a solid action plan that is rigorously followed, not just by procurement but by the stakeholders who hopefully have input to the plan. The last and probably most important element is having the right level of skilled resources.

10 Do we have the right skills?

The skills that allow procurement to really add value are all around sourcing of products and services. The skills and knowledge required will vary dependent of the category of spend and individual aptitude, but the right mix is required to be successful.

The starting point is to have quality data analyst expertise. Not everyone will be comfortable with downloading large amounts of transactional data and somehow making sense of all. Equally there is no point having someone who can crunch all the data without understanding what they are looking at.

Someone needs to be able to work with the business to determine the business requirement. The skills required in this area will vary greatly. For example, in aerospace companies it is very common to have whole engineering teams within the procurement function so that technical knowledge required understanding design requirements is on hand quickly. This will also be essential to perform true demand management in these instances. The opposite would be procuring more generic items like stationery where a high level of technical knowledge will not usually be required.

Market analysis skills will be required to explore the different possibilities of contracting that may be out there and the market constraints. For example, if you are buying spare parts it will be possible to buy parts from a distributor or the manufacturer or an alternate manufacturer. There will be a balance between price, service and product quality that will all need to be considered. Equally the whole category could be outsourced to a single management company. All these options have advantages and disadvantages depending on your exact situation, but it is important to have people who can think out of the box so that the maximum number of possibilities are considered. This will then become a major input to the formulation of a category strategy along with all the information compiled to date. The outcome of the strategy will be a description of a desired outcome in terms of how the goods are services should be delivered, preferred suppliers for the bidding process and a target level of savings.

Once the bid responses are received, it will be necessary to examine each in detail to understand exactly where and how savings are being offered. Different suppliers will do this in different ways. Some will offer simple price reductions, others will offer rebates and discounts dependent on volume of spend. But all the options will need to be evaluated so that a detailed negotiation strategy can be constructed for each supplier still in the game. Then the negotiator can do his or her job in way that tries to maximise the possibilities. Finally, once the deal is agreed it must be implemented and old agreements ended.

The right range of skills will deliver bumper benefits if applied to the right categories, but can take time to develop if there are gaps. But without these skills procurement cannot fulfil its potential.

About the Author

Brian Shanahan is the leader and founder of Informita. Informita was formed to assist companies in the areas of working capital and procurement, focusing on analytics, implementation and advisory. The team is there to support your working capital and procurement programmes from cradle to grave in a cost efficient and effective manner.

Before Informita, Brian spent 19 years in management consultancy, 5 years in financial accounting roles in the UK and 3 years in retail in Ireland. To date Brian has worked with over one hundred clients in 34 countries across 4 continents.

In the media, Brian has been quoted many times in the financial press in such publications as The Financial Times, CFO World, The Manufacturer, The Grocer, Finance Director, Euromoney, Accountancy Age, Financial i and The Evening Standard. Brian has also appeared on CNBC Europe's Power Lunch.

Contacts

If you would like more information on procurement please feel to contact us in the following ways:

Website: www.informita.com

Email: info@informita.com

Phone: +44-20-3286-4109

Twitter: @informita

Printed in Great Britain
by Amazon